THE BOOK OF THE

LORD NELSONS

A Photographic Accompaniment : 2

Notes by Richard Derry

Against the familiar backdrop of the Lifting Shop and newly in BR green, 30864 SIR MARTIN FROBISHER sits in Bournemouth shed yard, 19 July 1951. The meaning of 'BC' on the cylinder is anyone's guess... Photograph The Transport Treasury.

IRWELL PRESS Ltd.

ISBN 1-903266-71-8
ISBN 978-1-903266-71-7

Cover photo. 30864 SIR MARTIN FROBISHER, in apple green under all that grime, exits Bincombe North tunnel with a Bournemouth to Weymouth stopper on 31 May 1950. The up line climbs at 1 in 50, hence the sand drag to arrest any breakaway train. Photograph J.C. Flemons, The Transport Treasury.

First published in the United Kingdom in 2006
by Irwell Press Limited, 59A, High Street, Clophill,
Bedfordshire MK45 4BE
Printed by Newnorth Print, Bedford

THE BOOK OF THE LORD NELSONS
A Photographic Accompaniment : 2

Picture This
In the last few years we have seen the 'Book Of' series of locomotive studies develop into something of a library devoted to more and more of the principal BR express classes. Since 1997 there has been:
The Book of the BR Standards
The Book of the Coronation Pacifics
The Book of the Royal Scots
The Book of the Merchant Navy Pacifics
The Book of the Jubilee 4-6-0s
The Book of the West Country/Battle of Britain Pacifics
The Book of the Princess Royal Pacifics
The Book of the Patriot 4-6-0s
The Book of the BR Standards: 2
The Book of the A3 Pacifics
The Book of the Britannia Pacifics
The Book of the A4 Pacifics
The Book of the Lord Nelson 4-6-0s
The Book of the Schools 4-4-0s
The Book of the 9F 2-10-0s
The Book of the Stanier 2-6-0s

Beyond this a *de facto* journal has sprung up, in the shape of the *Photographic Accompaniments* to further celebrate these famous classes. These include, either published or projected:
The Britannia Pacifics,
A Photographic Accompaniment
The Coronation Pacifics,
A Photographic Accompaniment:1
The Coronation Pacifics,
A Photographic Accompaniment:2
The Coronation Pacifics,
A Photographic Accompaniment:3
The A4 Pacifics,
A Photographic Accompaniment:1
The A4 Pacifics,
A Photographic Accompaniment:2
The A4 Pacifics,
A Photographic Accompaniment:3
The A3 Pacifics,
A Photographic Accompaniment
The Lord Nelsons,
A Photographic Accompaniment:1
The Lord Nelsons,
A Photographic Accompaniment:2
The Schools,
A Photographic Accompaniment:1
The Princess Royals,
A Photographic Accompaniment:1

****

To briefly remind readers (you need those earlier books!) LORD NELSON emerged from Eastleigh in works grey in August 1926, a minor miracle of that engineer's art, that of forcing a significant increase in power with a minimal increase in weight.

Claimed as 'the most powerful passenger engine in the country' it was no accident that the inaugural public run of E850 LORD NELSON was on the Atlantic Coast Express. The new express class was designed to operate over all the main lines of the Southern and with an eye to the 'PR' value of it, the phrase '500 tons at 55mph' came into currency. Rather gloomily, given the maritime associations of the class, this claim was to sink without trace...
Ten more Lord Nelsons were delivered between June 1928 and April 1929; all were from Eastleigh to Order No.E157 (LORD NELSON had been E124) as follows:

E851 SIR FRANCIS DRAKE
E852 SIR WALTER RALEIGH
E853 SIR RICHARD GRENVILLE
E854 HOWARD OF EFFINGHAM
E855 ROBERT BLAKE
E856 LORD St VINCENT
E857 LORD HOWE
E858 LORD DUNCAN
E859 LORD HOOD
E860 LORD HAWKE

The last five Nelsons were built from September through to November 1929 (the 'E' went in 1930-1931):
E861 LORD ANSON
E862 LORD COLLINGWOOD
E863 LORD RODNEY
E864 SIR MARTIN FROBISHER
E865 SIR JOHN HAWKINS

It would be tedious to repeat even if space allowed all the detail variation discussed in the earlier books. Where they crop up I've usually drawn attention to them but in some instances a familiarity at least with the earlier descriptions will have been assumed.

Thanks, in especial, to Eric Youldon and Bryan Wilson. Also John Wickham, Bob Ratcliffe, Chris Hawkins, Ian Sixsmith, George Reeve and Martin Smith.

The following table is made up from a more comprehensive one first set out by D.W. Winkworth in *Maunsell's Nelsons* and subsequently amended in the light of later discoveries (personally communicated by Mr D.W. Winkworth and Mr E.S. Youldon, for which many thanks).

No.	850	851	852	853	854	855	856	857	858	859	860	861	862	863	864	865
Built	8/26	6/28	7/28c	9/28D	10/28	11/28	12/28	12/28R	2/29E	3/29E	4/29F	9/29	10/29K	10/29	11/29	11/29K
Tender modified	6/39	6/39	11/37	10/40	2/39	8/38	7/40	10/39	5/40	1/40	12/39	11/38	4/40	12/40	11/38	9/40
Flaman recorder	9/38	6/39	4/39	4/39	2/39	8/38	11/38	10/38	5/39	11/38	12/39	11/38	10/38	11/38	11/38H	6/39
Olive Green	-	-	4/39	-	2/39	11/38H	11/38H	-	5/39	5/39	-	11/38H	-	11/38	-	-
Lemaître exhaust	6/39	6/39	4/39	4/39	6/39	9/39L	8/39L	10/39	5/39	5/39	12/39	10/39L	5/39	6/39M	6/39L	6/39
Malachite Green	6/39	6/39	-	4/39	6/39	9/39	8/39	10/39	5/40	1/40	12/39	10/39	5/39	6/39	6/39	6/39
Modified cyl.	3/42	6/39N	3/40	2/58	11/46	12/40	7/40	10/39	1/51	12/46	12/39	8/43	4/40	-	5/48	9/40
Black livery	4/44	1/44	6/42	2/43	12/43	4/43	9/42	1/43	9/42	5/42	10/42	8/43	7/43	11/42	6/43	5/43
Malachite Green	11/46	11/46	3/47	6/47	11/46	5/47	6/46A	6/46	3/46	12/46	1/47	11/47A	8/48	9/46	2/47A	6/46
S. V. removed	11/48	1/49	3/49	11/48	6/49	2/49	4/48	12/49	1/48	1/48	11/48	11/47	8/48	11/47	5/48	8/48
BR renumbering	11/48	1/49	3/49	11/48	6/49B	2/49	4/48	12/49	6/48	2/49	11/48	5/48	8/48	8/49	5/48	8/48
BR Green	1/51	10/50	12/51	7/50	10/51	9/50	4/50	12/49	1/51	3/51	10/50	3/50	2/51	8/49	4/51	11/49
AWS gear	12/60	9/60	8/60	4/60	10/59	6/60	9/60	7/60	10/59	9/59	12/60	12/59	5/61	10/59	10/59	-
Speedometer	12/60	9/60	8/60	4/60	-	6/60	9/60	7/60	-	-	12/60	12/59	5/61	-	-	-
Withdrawn	8/62	12/61	2/62	3/62	9/61T	9/61	9/62	9/62	8/61	12/61	8/62	10/62	10/62	2/62	1/62	5/61T
Cut up	P	5/62	3/62	4/62	9/61	2/62	11/62	10/62	11/61	12/61	8/62	11/62	10/62	2/62	3/62	8/61

A – Apple-green livery acquired 30856 in 6/48, 30861/4 in 5/48
B – 'S' prefix 3/48
C – Six-wheel tender until 11/29 and Urie-type tender until 6/32
D – Six-wheel tender until 1/30 and Urie-type tender until 2/32
E – Urie-type tender until 6/32
F – Urie-type tender until 5/31 and fitted with longer boiler (no 860)
H – Fitted with large-diameter chimney and involved in exhaust experiments
K – Kylchap-type exhaust and double chimney fitted (no 862 in 8/34 and no 865 in 3/38)
L – Fitted with standard Lemaître exhaust and large-diameter chimney
M – Fitted with large-diameter chimney and involved in exhaust experiments 6/38
N – Non-standard modified cylinders
P – Preserved
R – Non-Belpaire boiler (no 1063) fitted from 1/37 to 9/41 and from 1/43 to 2/45
T – Tender 1007 from no 30854 transferred to no 30921 and tender 1012 from no 30865 to no 30912
S.V.- Snifting Valves

When you had the country's most powerful locomotive it made sense to exploit the publicity potential. A favourite device of British railway companies was the 'David & Goliath' image, and an effective one it was too. So the Southern wheeled out dear old GLADSTONE, the Brighton 0-4-2 and this was the result (prior to actual exhibition of course) in Nine Elms shed yard in the summer of 1926. LORD NELSON was in fact frequently on show and was with GLADSTONE again, at Brighton, in May 1927. Its first revenue earning service was the 11am boat train from Victoria on 16 May 1927.

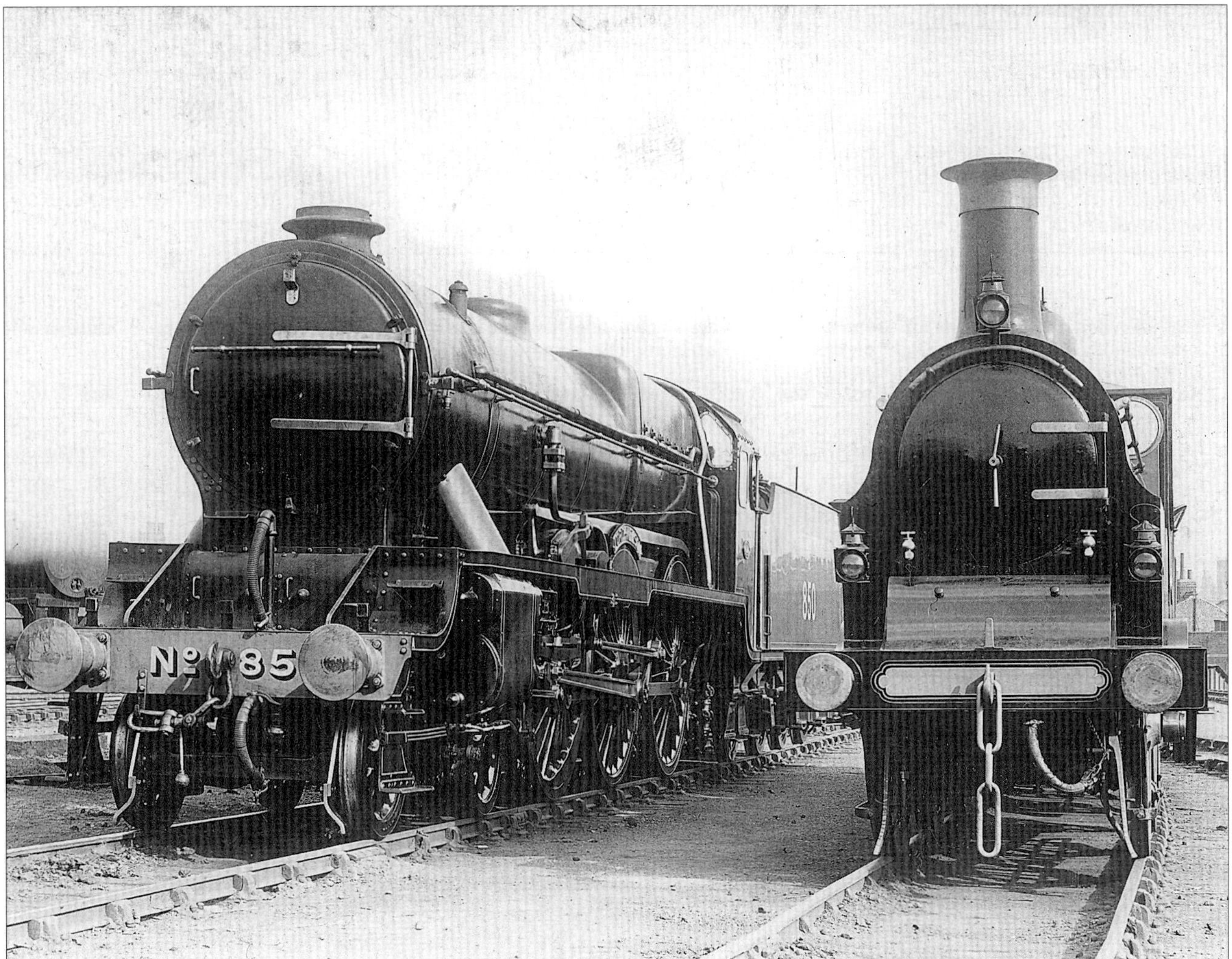

A new LORD NELSON, side on at Stewarts Lane. It might seem just another 4-6-0 to us now, and not a particularly modern one at that but in the 1920s this was the very forefront of express working. It was huge! That hefty firebox, surprisingly, was derived from the Maunsell N mogul design, enlarged up to the loading gauge limits.

Out on the loose, 'leaving Victoria' (those trees are a bit suspicious though) 'with the 9am down continental boat train, Whit Sunday'.

LORD NELSON during its test period on the Western Section, at Nine Elms with the indicator shelter fitted. This looks like the same picture as that on page 2 of *The Book of the Lord Nelson 4-6-0s* and page 3 of *Accompaniment:1* but isn't quite. The driver has the same jutting-jaw pose but there was clearly a sequence, which is good enough excuse to reproduce this image once more... After running in and its exhibition at various places LORD NELSON, with its indicator apparatus, was put on a variety of expresses, most memorably on the sixteen coach Atlantic Coast Express in April 1927. LORD NELSON easily achieved Maunsell's goal of 1,500 horse power and the aim of '500 tons at 55mph' seemed in the bag.

The grate area of the new locomotive was the largest of any 4-6-0 in the country, apart from the GWR Kings. The enormous 'look' of LORD NELSON owed a lot to the fact that only a minimal amount of firebox penetrated rearward into the cab. In fact what we have here is not quite what you'd think, for this is the famous impersonation of LORD NELSON, when 861 LORD ANSON was spruced up and disguised as 850 for the Liverpool & Manchester celebrations of 1930.

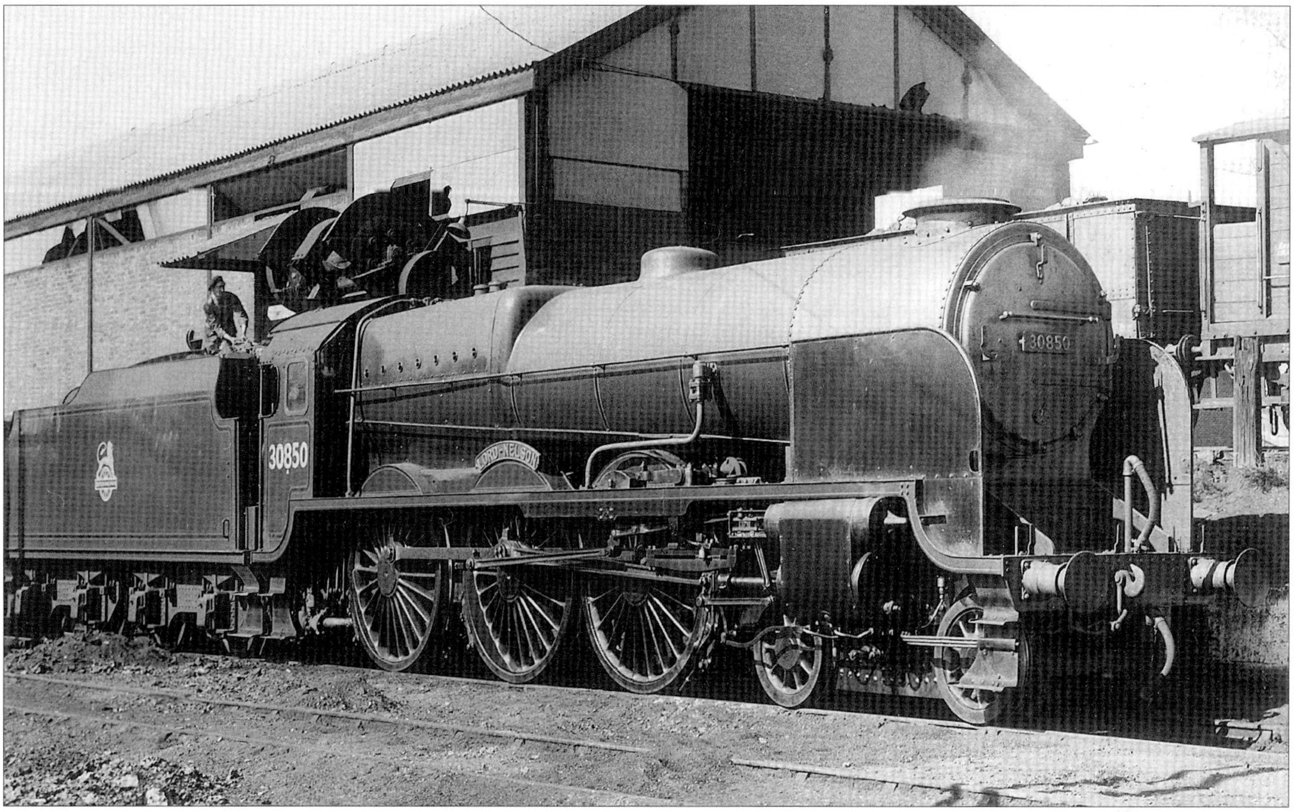

A BR green 30850 LORD NELSON at the coaling stage at Eastleigh, with wide chimney but snifting valves gone. In 1959 there was 'an occurrence without precedent' (according to *Trains Illustrated*) when LORD NELSON appeared in St David's station, Exeter, working in with a Royal Legion special from Southampton, bound for Newton Abbot. Early 10 inch number.

30850 LORD NELSON at Basingstoke in June 1956 with a train a long way indeed from the concept of '500 tons at 50mph'.

A much more appropriate loading, at Battledown on 4 September 1959 on an up 'boat' from Southampton, having gone over the flyover. Photograph J. Robertson, The Transport Treasury.

To an extent, the Nelsons found themselves the 'second string' locomotives on the Southampton and Bournemouth lines after the Southern became replete with Pacifics and its expression could go as far as this, LORD NELSON heading a pick-up goods at St Denys on 13 August 1956. Yet we should not make too much of this, for the Southern was never much bothered with class distinctions. It made the best possible use of locomotives whenever it could and even Merchant Navy rosters included stoppers and goods daily. Note clear outline where steam pipe casing had protruded through the smoke deflectors. Photograph J. Robertson, The Transport Treasury.

Maybe it was, however, that the Southern had the perfect mixed traffic tool! Here is the premier Nelson with a substantial Waterloo-Bournemouth train near Brockenhurst, 26 June 1954. Photograph R.C. Riley, The Transport Treasury.

Still majestic, 30850 stands raring to go, by the look of it, on the coaling plant roads at Nine Elms on 17 August 1956. 30865 SIR JOHN HAWKINS stands behind. The enormous belpaire firebox, so distinctive a feature was in fact only 18 inches longer than a King Arthur but it was this box that lay at the heart of the Nelsons' problems, so far as working them was concerned. The engines demanded rather more skill in firing, because of the split level grate. Men didn't take to them, yet years later the same crews (or their successors) took split level grate BR Standards in their stride. Photograph J. Robertson, The Transport Treasury.

An unusual view, 850 LORD NELSON on the newish stall road off the turntable at Bournemouth shed. The loco is in Bulleid livery but still has Maunsell cylinders – the period is thus between May 1939 and January 1942. Photograph Butts Junction Collection.

Keeping company at Eastleigh about 1960, where the class was long concentrated. They had only ever been at a handful of sheds, the hope being that men could handle them often enough to get the hang of it. Photograph Butts Junction Collection.

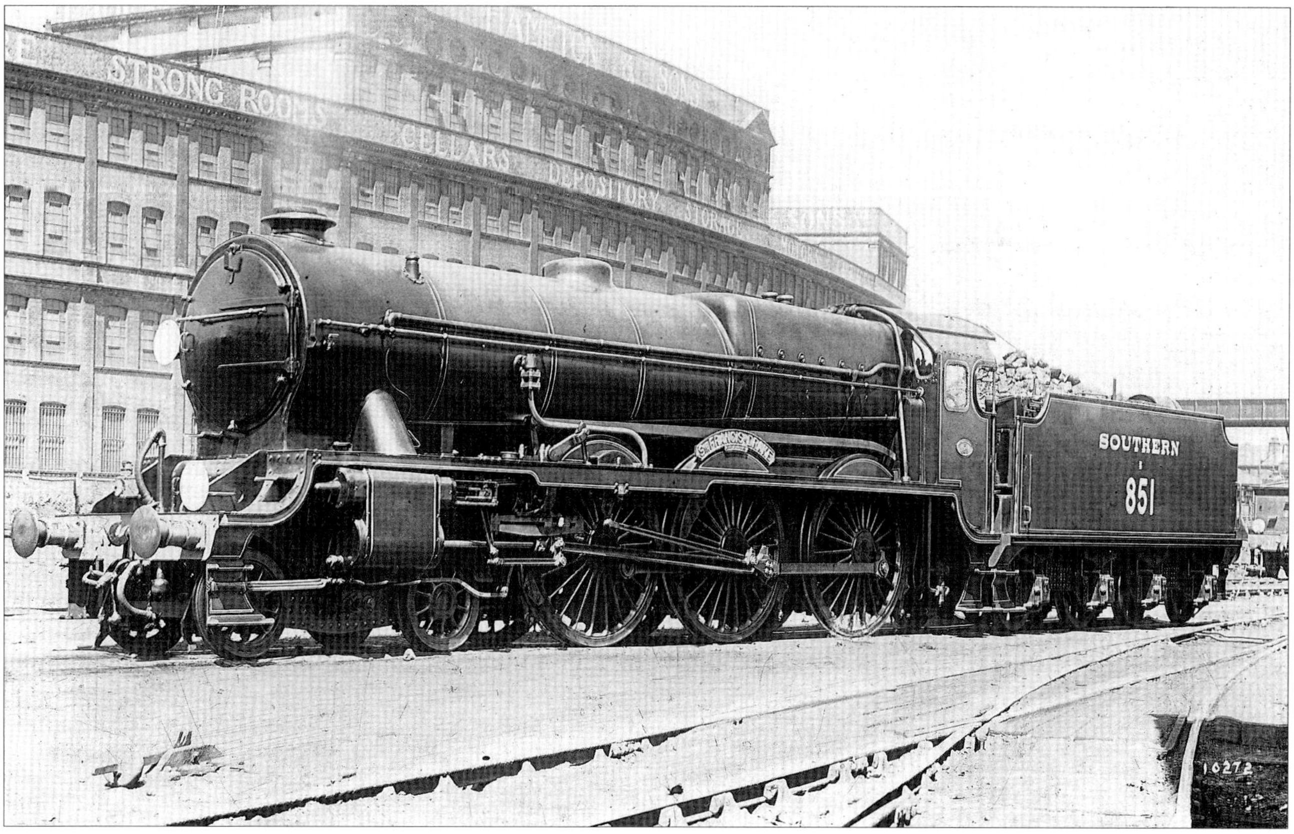

E851 SIR FRANCIS DRAKE in original sage green at Stewarts Lane with the famous Depository behind. The loco spent most of the 1930s at Stewarts Lane, moving to Nine Elms (there could hardly be two sheds more closely contiguous in the country) in 1940. A German rocket would later radically alter the background outline in this familiar scene.

851 SIR FRANCIS DRAKE, in malachite, emerges from Fisherton tunnel, Salisbury, with the up Atlantic Coast Express about 1939. That's more like it! It's easy to give the impression that the Nelsons lost their prestige from the time they departed the Eastern Section for Western climes. It was a 'sideways move' though, because they became the mainstay of the Bournemouth expresses and to a lesser extent the Salisbury workings. Their 'retreat into the shadows' as Eric Youldon has put it, by chance really coincided with the application of the BR green, so dull compared to the malachite. They continued to play an important, if somewhat less exalted, role.

In malachite at Bournemouth Central; this is the first application, in 1939 and truly effective it was. Now with LeMaître exhaust but still with snifting valves on the smokebox. The enlarged tender sides got a bit warped in later years but when in perfect order, as here, were very impressive indeed.

'E' prefix gone, SIR FRANCIS DRAKE is down at Dover in the 1930s on a boat job, the sort of work for which the Nelsons were very largely intended. What D.W. Winkworth called, with commendable understatement, 'an unflattering decision' was taken in 1936 when the new 'Night Ferry' sleeper was declared *too heavy* for the Nelsons. The Southern then employed pairs of 4-4-0s.

Glistening in the first malachite, at Bournemouth in 1939. From the late 1930s, when malachite and olive green began to appear, the Nelson livery afterwards becomes the Vale of Tears described in 'The Book Of'. When you add in lining variations, as Bradley puts it, there were 'so many variations of the theme that the only features common to all were the large gilt buffer beam numerals, SOUTHERN on the tenders and cab numerals'.

30851 SIR FRANCIS DRAKE at Eastleigh shed. The engine was curious in at least a couple of respects. The original bogie frame arrangement on the Nelsons was found to be unsatisfactory and the side frames were altered from this curved outline to a straight one – as evidenced at length in the two previous volumes. SIR FRANCIS, somehow, retained its original bogie and was the only one to do so. Secondly, it had got new cylinders in 1939 but 'a misunderstanding' meant 8 inch instead of 10 inch piston valves were fitted. It thus retained the piano front to the end; 30863 did too, but that was because it never got new cylinders at all. Just to confuse us though, despite the piano front and original short smokebox there are no steam pipes visible through the smoke deflectors...

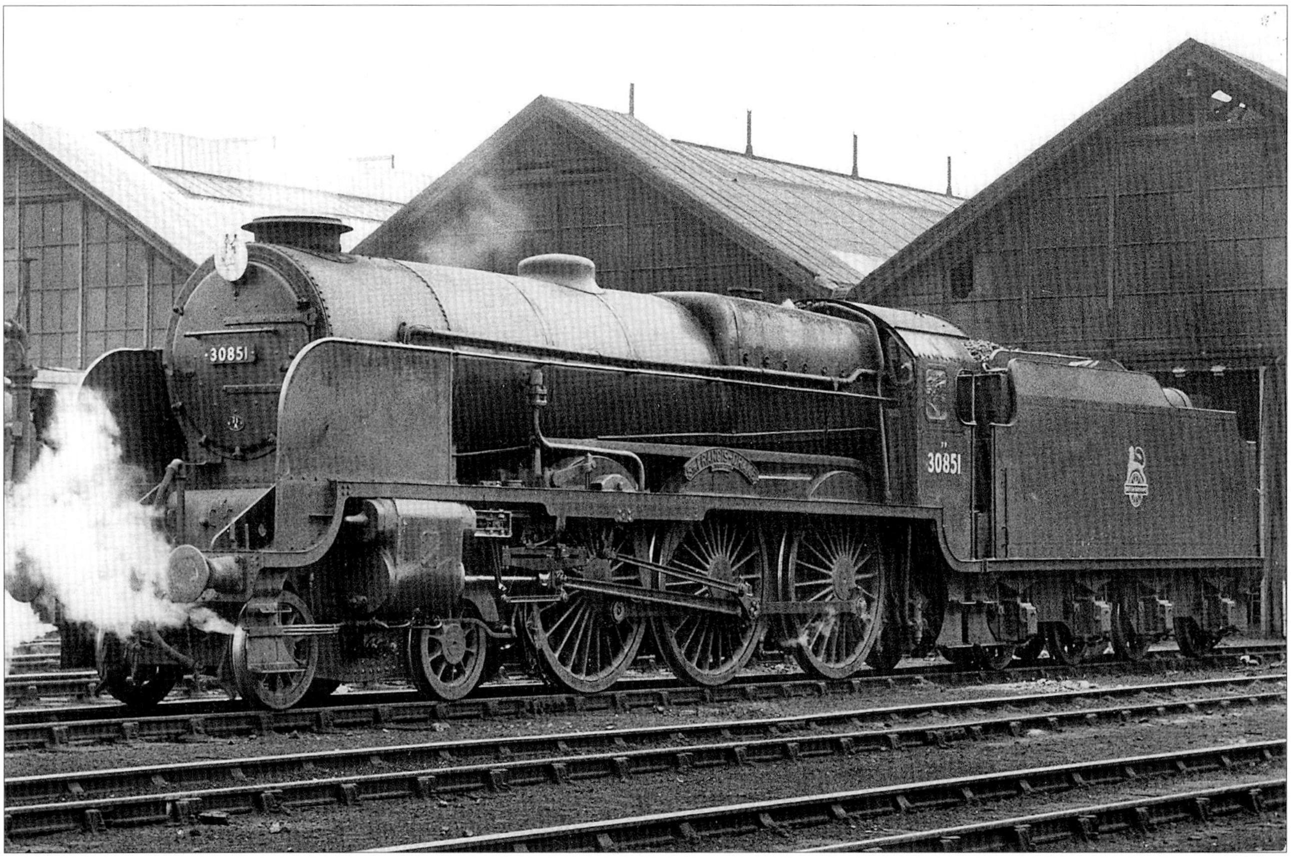

E852 SIR WALTER RALEIGH at Dover in original condition; along with E853 it came out with this inappropriate six wheel tender, which served to make that vast boiler look even more massive. Original bogie frame, snifting valves and the projecting lamp irons, the latter making the indicator discs a sore trial for a man looking out.

As good an illustration as any of the drawbacks of the original lamp irons. They were moved inside to the smokebox door which meant removing the handle – afterwards you opened the door using the lamp iron. This is E852 SIR WALTER RALEIGH at Tonbridge with, presumably, a boat train, on 18 August 1928. Photograph H.C. Casserley, courtesy R.M. Casserley.

852 SIR WALTER RALEIGH at Woking in May 1936. The Nelsons had the front number painted on the buffer beam with 'Nº.' on the other side of the drawhook. The 'Nº.' was dropped for the 'E' prefix only to reappear when the 'E' in turn was done away with in 1931. This time, as here, the 'Nº.' had the underline set higher, with a dot underneath it. See how the lamp irons are now on the smokebox door.

852 SIR WALTER RALEIGH looking gorgeous at Eastleigh in 1939, in olive green with the full green deflectors that were confined to this one and 859. It got new cylinders the following year; these are the old ones, so the steam pipes still project through the deflectors.

852 SIR WALTER RALEIGH in Clapham cutting; post-war malachite and a leafy common. Photograph R.A. Morant Collection.

853 SIR RICHARD GRENVILLE at Orpington in full cry with a boat working. It's in perfect, shining condition but the high lamp iron has appeared on the buffer beam. This was to serve for the smokebox position lamp, without waiting for the those irons themselves to be brought in. The disc on the tall lamp iron counted as if it were on the projecting iron. From the cab rearwards 'the most powerful locomotive in the country' is let down somewhat by that six wheel 4,000 gallon tender.

853 SIR RICHARD GRENVILLE with a down Dover train near Chelsfield. It has the Urie 5,000 gallon tender fitted in February 1930 and the tall lamp iron. It also proves that the middle lamp irons did not pass to the smokebox door as a direct consequence of the fitting of smoke deflectors. Photograph R.S. Carpenter Collection.

30853 SIR RICHARD GRENVILLE at Raynes Park with a down Bournemouth West express; EMU in Platform 3 on a headcode 'V' Kingston 'roundabout' job. Post-war malachite, with BRITISH RAILWAYS on the tender, this was one of Bournemouth's top link locos, kept in immaculate condition. Note superb Bulleid deep-sided stock.

30853 SIR RICHARD GRENVILLE crossing Canute Road to enter the docks at Southampton with an up boat train. All the Nelsons finished up at Eastleigh, under Shedmaster Stephen Townroe. He avoided Pacifics for 'the boats' (as they were called) because they 'were less easy to keep quiet and smoke-free in the Docks'. Cars were barely known back then and there were no gates or flashing lights, merely a simple TRAINS CROSS HERE and two blokes with flags, like this. SIR RICHARD retained Maunsell cylinders until March 1958. Photograph E. Trotter, The Transport Treasury.

It is August 1960 now, at Lymington Junction and SIR RICHARD GRENVILLE has the new cylinders and thus the flat front under the smokebox and steam pipes no longer penetrate the smoke deflectors. It carries the contemporary livery of grey grime but has acquired AWS and speedometer. It has the first BR emblem on the tender, 're-acquired' as a result of a tender change.

A Nelson in all the original glory of the class, E854 HOWARD OF EFFINGHAM at what looks like Stewarts Lane. Note the intricate lining and the 'A' power classification behind the buffer beam.

854 HOWARD OF EFFINGHAM, the 'E' jettisoned and now with smoke deflectors, at Victoria in July 1936. Observe the change in the bogie frame outline. If the slidebar looks familiar, it's because Bulleid adopted it for his Pacifics.

854 was unique in receiving Bulleid livery in February 1939 in conjunction with its Maunsell chimney. A LeMaître chimney was gained in June 1939; here is HOWARD OF EFFINGHAM a little before that, at Stewarts Lane on 7 May 1939. Photograph J.D. Darby.

Shawford, 21 July 1952. 30854 HOWARD OF EFFINGHAM, hauling the 3.24pm Southampton Central to Waterloo had come to grief the day before when it derailed at catch points at the end of the up relief road south of Shawford. The reason was a misreading of signals but happily no one was hurt. Photograph J.R. Fairman.

855 ROBERT BLAKE at Knockholt in 1936 with the mid-week Golden Arrow. Several Nelsons, like this one, spent most of the 1930s on the Eastern Section boat workings, making many fine performances despite what is said about unhappy crews. So it was that in the history of the class they were concentrated at a very restricted number of sheds for much of the time; Battersea and Nine Elms before the Second World War, then Nine Elms and Bournemouth with a brief stay at Dorchester for two in 1954. From 1949 migration to Eastleigh commenced and all were there by the end of the 1950s. It was a situation more or less unique for a principal express class.

855 was one of two Lord Nelsons (the other was 852) that received a modified tender while still decked out in Maunsell livery. ROBERT BLAKE ran in this form from August to November 1938.

855 ROBERT BLAKE, still on boat working but now in Bulleid livery with the modified tender, fitted in 1938.

855 ROBERT BLAKE at Clapham Junction, on what looks like empty stock. All the tenders got this 'distorted' look in latter years, where the welds and framing from the 'self-trimming' modifications of the 1930s started to show their age. Short-lived right-hand lion emblem on tender. Photograph The Transport Treasury.

856 LORD ST VINCENT at Waterloo in 1937. Note modified bogie framing – now with 'straight' lower edge. It did not get new cylinders and thus lose the piano front and steam pipes until 1940.

856 LORD ST VINCENT on a boat train at Dover in the 1930s. The nature of the services did not help the Nelsons' cause. There were simply not enough Dover/Folkestone services (excluding summer weekends) to allow for double trips between London and the coast in a day; there were only five each way per day and they were tied, moreover, to shipping times. So mileages could never be prodigious.

In BR garb about 1953, at Eastleigh, now its home shed.

At Eastleigh, 30856 LORD ST VINCENT, with ten inch figures, catches the light on 17 May 1953. The little curved form, like a miniature splasher alongside the front splasher, was a hinged cover that could be lifted at the open end so that the junction of pivot, radius rod and expansion link underneath could be inspected. That crosshead and slidebar design was later used on the Schools and, as mentioned, was duly adopted by Bulleid for his Pacifics. The D15 tender nicely contrasts large and small emblems. Photograph L.R. Freeman, The Transport Treasury.

30856 LORD ST VINCENT with a train at Brockenhurst, 24 May 1953. That flat front consequent on the fitting of new cylinders made for a very different appearance. Photograph R.C. Riley, The Transport Treasury.

30856 LORD ST VINCENT at Eastleigh, 15 August 1956. The Nelsons had sanding only to the front of the forward driving wheels; the circular filling cap is on the running plate above the crosshead. Photograph J. Robertson, The Transport Treasury.

857 LORD HOWE before its transformation, in front of the grand old Depository at Stewarts Lane; Maunsell green livery. Another hindrance to intensive working of the Nelsons on the Eastern Section were the operational restrictions imposed at Holborn Viaduct; only the D and E 4-4-0s could go there, effectively ruling out the use of the big 4-6-0s on the early morning trains and the late night vans/newspapers.

857 LORD HOWE with the curious taper boiler at Waterloo, October 1937. It had been fitted in January and the engine went to Nine Elms and then Stewarts Lane. The boiler was removed in September 1941 and was carried again from January 1943 to February 1945. It was said to steam better except when driven hard. Further experiments were needed with the blastpipe and chimney arrangements but Maunsell retired and Bulleid evinced little or no interest. The taper boiler was no.1063 and its purpose was to gain experience as a prelude to the introduction of a Pacific express passenger locomotive and a goods 4-8-0. It had a round top firebox, combustion chamber and 'Sinuflo' superheater and had an extended row of washout plugs along the firebox for the combustion chamber. For several years it was a feature of the boiler dump at Eastleigh works, finally going for scrap in 1952. Note 'cranked' smoke deflectors, low dome because of the scale of the boiler and single snifting valve behind the chimney.

857 LORD HOWE with the taper boiler at Vauxhall in August 1937; that would make the Pullman the Bournemouth Belle.

30857 LORD HOWE runs into Bournemouth West in April 1957 – an easy trundle downhill from Bournemouth West Junction into the station. The class probably lasted longer than it might because of the peak nature of operating on the Southern. Despite all the Pacifics and King Arthurs, on summer Saturdays especially, everything had to be thrown into the fray. Photograph R.C. Riley, The Transport Treasury.

858 LORD DUNCAN at Chelsfield with a down Dover boat train. Plain top chimney.

Just two Lord Nelsons ran with BR number and SOUTHERN on the tender, 30858 and 30859. This one has Maunsell cylinders so is 30858 LORD DUNCAN. It is climbing Upwey bank with an up train around September 1948 Photograph R.A. Morant Collection

858 LORD DUNCAN sweeps past the splendid new housing at Petts Wood in August 1938, with a continental train Dover to Victoria. Piano front, original cylinders, tender not modified.

30858 LORD DUNCAN, still a Nine Elms engine (it did not gravitate to the Eastleigh pool until 1958) in everyday grime at Eastleigh on 20 September 1951 with the 9.30am Waterloo-Bournemouth. A typical duty during the long twilight of the class.

In original state at Stewarts Lane shed, E859 LORD HOOD in that glorious Maunsell green and all original features including Urie tender, projecting lamp irons and the rest. The SR policy (how could it really be otherwise?) was to allocate locos for the days of 'maximum use' which inevitably meant a number would be spare for some periods. During the 1934-35 winter, for instance, 853, 856, 863 and 864 were all stored at Stewarts Lane.

E859 LORD HOOD, still with the Urie tender, at Chelsfield with a down 'continental'.

859 LORD HOOD, now with straight sided tender, on show at Sutton in September 1934.

859 LORD HOOD down at the docks, off a working at Dover. LORD HOOD had 6ft 3in driving wheels instead of the 6ft 7in of the rest, apparently to determine if this would suit the loco more to heavily graded routes like the LSW west of Salisbury. It had originally been proposed that the wheels for LORD HOOD should be 6ft 0in, for use on the *Eastern* Section but this would have meant too much extra work. Whatever, there seems to have been no discernible difference in working and LORD HOOD was regarded as indistinguishable from the others. Try as you might, you'll be hard pressed to actually spot the difference.

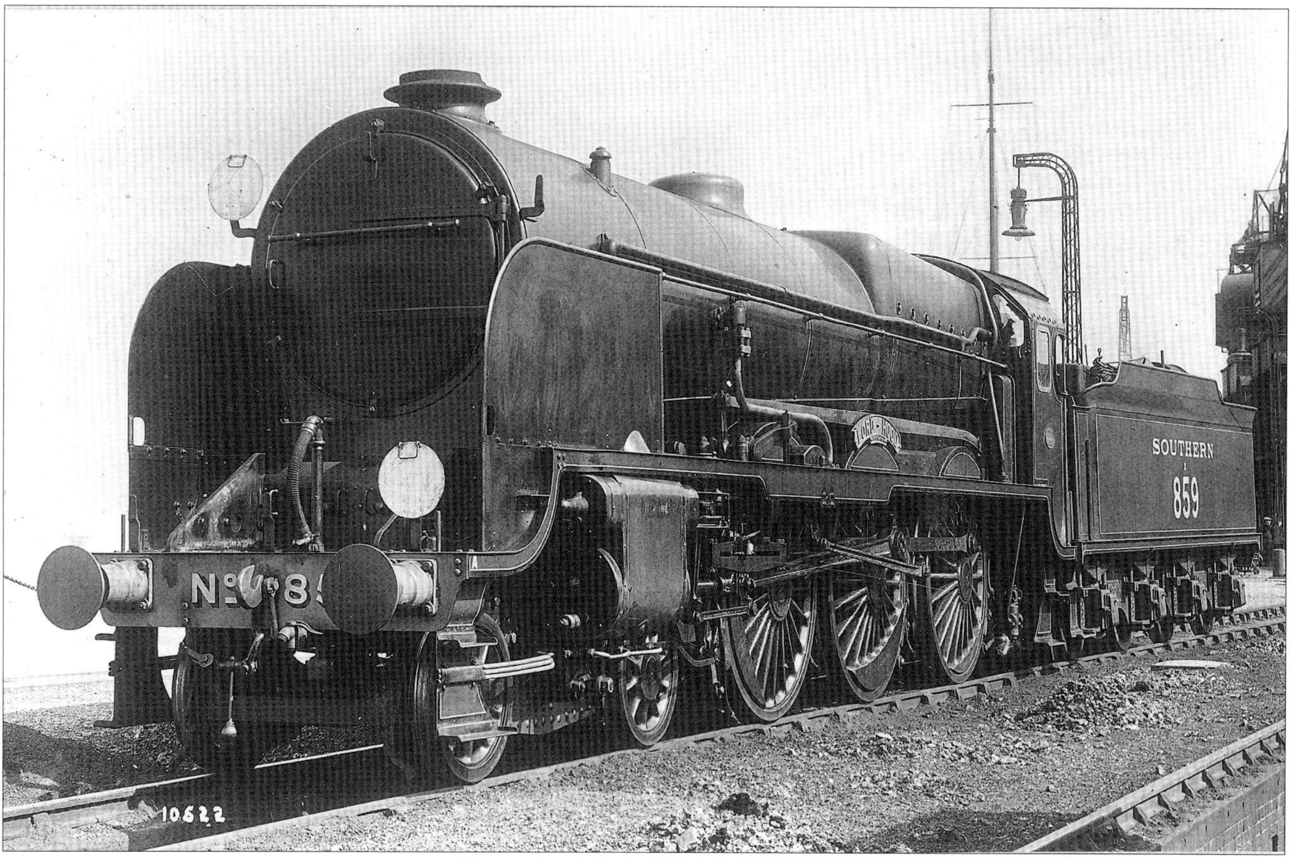

30859 LORD HOOD near Worting Junction, milepost 50¼, with a down Bournemouth express on the Down Southampton line.

E860 LORD HAWKE in original condition at Nine Elms, so scintillating that even the term 'exhibition finish' would barely be sufficient. It was the last in the main 'production run' of ten, E851-E860 and the last to appear without smoke deflectors.

860 LORD HAWKE, at Eastleigh shed in 1936. Maunsell had it built with a longer boiler, its tubes longer by ten inches than the 13ft 9in of the others. No increased performance was to be found and the notion was, as Townroe puts it, 'a lemon'. LORD HAWKE, it can be seen, had a flat front from the first, though it is wrong to say it never had the 'piano'; there was a period in the 1930s when 860 ran with a standard LN boiler, when it would have had the piano front. The boiler itself, no.860, was used on other Nelsons in later years.

30860 LORD HAWKE at Eastleigh on an up fast; it spent more or less its entire life on the Western Section. The notice on the right forbids walking between station and shed via the tracks. Photograph J. Robertson, The Transport Treasury.

Two sides of 30860 LORD HAWKE on the ash roads at Nine Elms about 1957. AWS and speedometer have yet to appear. The Nelsons were without doubt wonderful to look at and, however 'relegated' they were after 1949, could heave on its way any summer Saturday train that the operating people could throw at them. It had been a glorious period after 1945 when Bournemouth had ten and Nine Elms six. Then, they were front rank motive power on the Bournemouth line, until Bournemouth started to get Pacifics in 1949. Standard Lord Nelson boiler in both views.

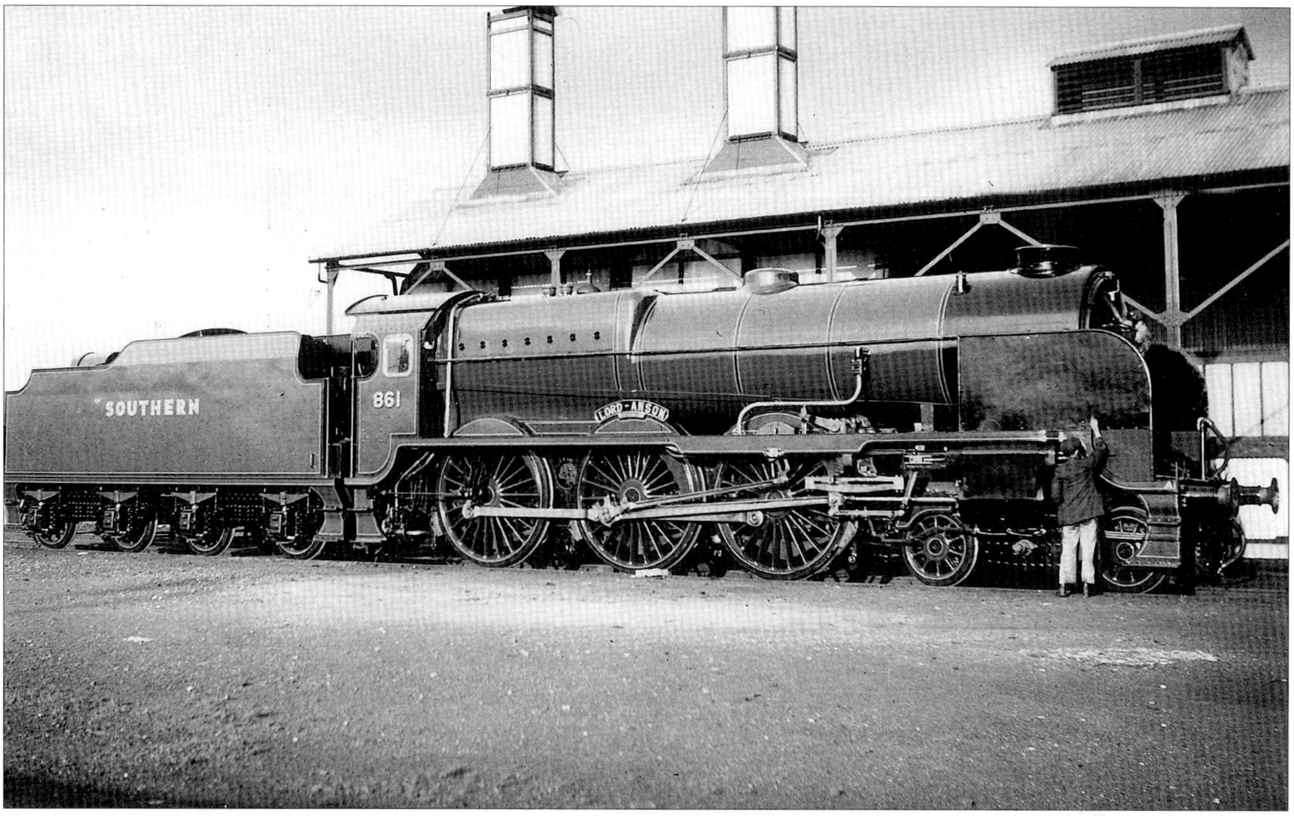

861 LORD ANSON on 14 November 1938, newly outshopped in olive green. This one, and the remaining four, appeared new with smoke deflectors. An errant speck of dirt is perhaps being removed from the said smoke deflector by the Driver while it looks like the Fireman is doing something at the front. You can only marvel at the intricacy of the livery detail. This is Eastleigh Works though what part I know not. The giant vents imply a steaming shed or something like it. LORD ANSON has the stovepipe chimney and the beautiful livery applied to four Nelsons, 855, 856, 861 and 863. This was olive green, cream and dark green lining, plain black cylinders and smoke deflectors with nine inch gilt and shadow number and nine inch SOUTHERN on the tender.

Charging along with a boat train, 861 LORD ANSON is at Bromley on 18 February 1939. It went to the Liverpool & Manchester celebrations in 1930 (there always seems to be this sort of instance in the history of express classes on the Big Four in the 1920s and 1930s) disguised as LORD NELSON. Photograph H.C. Casserley, courtesy R.M. Casserley.

Poole, and a solid BR Nelson drifts past with the usual impressive train in June 1955. LORD ANSON had taken part in coal consumption trials under Bulleid in 1946, along with 21C14 NEDERLAND LINE and 789 SIR GUY. As 'The Book Of' puts it: ***LORD ANSON returned a little under 45lbs per mile, which was hardly remarkable, for it was what was expected of a Nelson at the time (Winkworth). Such figures are what you make of them of course, and Bradley uses the same figure to make a fascinating historical point, given the associations of the Lord Nelson design with that of the Royal Scots – LORD ANSON's figures were almost exactly comparable to the LM's 46154 THE HUSSAR in the BR locomotive exchanges eighteen months or so later.***

The Nelsons found regular work to Oxford from Bournemouth; this is 30861 LORD ANSON at Hinksey South on 15 August 1959. Photograph R.C. Riley, The Transport Treasury.

862 LORD COLLINGWOOD with its distinctive double chimney, which had made its appearance in August 1934. It was a modified Kylchap twin exhaust arrangement of the in-line type and while this was widely successful it never 'worked' for LORD COLLINGWOOD. Once again, on a single technical instance it is worth quoting the original 'Book Of'; this is what Dr W.A. Tuplin wrote in *Railway World* in April 1959: *It is hard to believe that anyone really thought that these changes could possibly make any perceptible difference to performance and they certainly did not. It is significant that the one thing that was obviously at fault* [he meant the firebox] *was not altered, even in the special boilers, and so one is inclined to believe that Maunsell was trying not to put the Nelsons right but rather to prove how good the original design was by showing that no change that anyone suggested could effect any improvement.* It certainly altered the whole look of the locomotive, and hardly for the better... or did it?

Bounding round that line at Petts Wood, August 1938, LORD COLLINGWOOD is on the 2pm 'continental' Victoria to Dover. In May the following year the double kylchap would give way to the wide diameter LeMaître chimney.

Malachite 30862 LORD COLLINGWOOD approaching Worgret Junction on 30 June 1950 (BRITISH RAILWAYS on tender) with a five coach portion of a train for Dorchester and Weymouth. That would be the Swanage branch going off to the right. I've been accused of 'denigrating' these wonderful locomotives but this is way off. The fact is that circumstances conspired to relegate them somewhat from the front rank of working. It was the peculiar circumstances of motive power supply and the exaggerated traffic peaks of the Southern that saw this come about, rather than any inherent shortcomings. Photograph J.C. Flemons, The Transport Treasury.

30862
122

30862 LORD COLLINGWOOD in BR green, at Surbiton. It's slightly startling to read Townroe's verdict that the Nelsons were obsolescent even in 1948 'and quite obsolescent alongside the excellent BR Class 5s, easily serviced and maintained'. Photograph R.A. Morant Collection.

Stirring action for 30862 LORD COLLINGWOOD; this is quite late on in the 1950s, for 30862 has got its second BR emblem but not yet AWS. The 50¼ milepost reveals that we are near Worting – see LORD HOOD earlier.

Eastleigh, true 'home' of the Nelsons, with LORD COLLINGWOOD looking near-perfect on 25 July 1956. BR power classification '7P' above the number. Photograph Brian Morrison.

30863 LORD RODNEY lays smoke across the railway leaving Basingstoke for Waterloo, 24 June 1956. Photograph R.C. Riley, The Transport Treasury.

863 LORD RODNEY got its first big chimney in June 1938 and retained Maunsell livery, being the only Nelson to do so. It ran thus until painting in olive green in November 1938. Both these views date from July 1938, at Brookwood and Waterloo respectively.

Some rarely-available tender detail in May 1952; 30863 LORD RODNEY at Clapham Junction, doubtless while working empty stock. A heap of coal typically where it shouldn't be! Photograph G.A. Hookham.

The Battledown Flyover on 4 September 1959. 30863 LORD RODNEY heads a Southampton boat train for Waterloo. Photograph J. Robertson, The Transport Treasury.

864 SIR MARTIN FROBISHER was another unique Nelson for a short time insofar that its first new livery involved retention of the Maunsell (sage) green with the new markings. This pairing was applied from January to June 1939; SIR MARTIN is here on display at Brookwood on 23 April that year. Photograph R. Blencowe Collection.

30864 SIR MARTIN FROBISHER leaving Southampton Central; this would be the first half of the 1950s, given the ten inch number. Photograph E.E. Smith.

A visit to the Western, 2 March 1957. 30864 SIR MARTIN FROBISHER has worked in to Oxford earlier, turned at the WR shed and is now ready to depart back south to Bournemouth. Photograph Dr G.D. Parkes.

Something of a puzzle, this one, the date given as 1 August 1952; fearing nought, the money has to be on 30864 SIR MARTIN FROBISHER, its tender and smoke deflector gashes matching the loco's condition for 1952. Photograph J. Robertson, The Transport Treasury.

Double chimney 865 SIR JOHN HAWKINS comes under Newbury Road bridge through Whitchurch station (between Basingstoke and Andover) on 7 April 1938 with the down Atlantic Coast Express.

Bottom left. 865 SIR JOHN HAWKINS in the shed yard at Dover; original cylinders, snifting valves and the chance for a good look at the single sanding pipe and filler. It's worth expounding somewhat further on the curious matter of the Nelson replacement cylinders. This is possible courtesy of notes prepared long ago by Eric Youldon for *Southern Express*, the journal of the Merchant Navy Locomotive Preservation Society, and endorsed by Stephen Townroe: 'It is often thought that the large chimneys and the new cylinders with 10in valves were simultaneously incorporated in the Lord Nelsons, but in practice the situation was rather different. All sixteen locomotives received the new chimneys and multiple-jet blast pipes in 1938/39, but the new pattern cylinders were introduced much more slowly, as follows:

2 locos in 1939 (857/60)
5 locos in 1940 (852/55/56/62/65)
1 loco in 1942 (850)
1 loco in 1943 (861)
2 locos in 1946 (854/59)
1 loco in 1948 (30864)
1 loco in 1951 (30858)
1 loco in 1958 (30853)
Total 14

'This left two engines unaltered in this respect, namely 30851/63 and these carried their cylinders with 8in valves through to scrapping. It will be noticed that whereas nine examples had been altered in four years, it took a further 15 years to alter the next five! The reason for this is not hard to find as the new pattern cylinders failed to make any improvement that was observable in practice. 'Nelsons' with old and new pattern cylinders worked turn and turn about and no one minded or even noticed the difference except sharp-eyed observers who were aware that 10in valves involved a slightly extended smoke box and steam pipe casings no longer protruded below the deflectors. It would appear that after initial enthusiasm had worn off, renewals took place only when cylinders genuinely required replacement.

'The simple truth is there was nothing wrong with the original Nelson cylinders. Whatever other defects the engines may have had, the cylinder proportions were correct for all the work the engines were likely to perform. The same design of cylinder was used in the Schools class, and these were never altered nor has anyone suggested they should have been.

'It seems strange in retrospect, that although the Lord Nelsons were subjected to numerous modifications in Maunsell's time, the feature which was their main weakness – a firebox design which made for difficult firing – was left severely alone except in the case of the experimental boiler carried for a few years by 857. This boiler was fitted with a thermic syphon by Bulleid in 1943, but after two years' service was removed and after languishing at Eastleigh was cut up in the early 1950s. From all accounts 857 was something of a lame duck during the period 1943-45.

'A further Nelson modification which has never been much publicised concerns the double chimneys. 862 was thus equipped in 1934 and this experiment appeared to interest Bulleid as before he started to install the LeMaître multiple-jet blastpipe he gave 865 (in 1938) a double chimney. 865 was the 'four beat' Nelson and 862 and 865 were then put to work on the Bournemouth line and a check was made on their timekeeping and fuel consumptions. 865 proved to be much the better timekeeper but burned more coal (which was to be expected). Nothing more was done with double chimneys on the Southern and both engines soon acquired the LeMaître arrangement along with the others.'

865 SIR JOHN HAWKINS at Waterloo with its double chimney is actually a rare subject to find in photographs. It ran with it from March 1938 to June 1939 and the chimney had a different top profile from the otherwise similar one on 862.

Closeted on shed, 30865 SIR JOHN HAWKINS at Bournemouth, 6 April 1957. Photograph D.W. Winkworth.

THE BLACK BOX... THE BLACK BOX... THE BLACK BOX...

Sins of omission and commission creep in; some take a while to be uncovered and the idea is that, as these books continue, matters should be updated as we go along. In *The Book of the Lord Nelson 4-6-0s* the most egregious shortcomings concerned LORD HOWE on page 6. At the top of course, the engine is not at Salisbury but Dover. This was due to procedural deficiencies here in the sprawling Irwell Press empire (the technical bit, in the basement). The caption was inexplicably mangled to imply both views were Salisbury. The author knew it was Dover of course. To compound all this, on page 54 the same picture is used when the intention was to have a slightly different one, taken at the same time with a different engine in the background. But you get the meaning...

In 'The Book Of' several locations were simply not known – the loco after all, is the subject. Mr J. Wickham of Ramsgate and Mr R.P. Stevenson of Folkestone recognised 857 on page 55 as Sydenham Hill and 862 on page 72 (lower) as Earlsfield. SIR FRANCIS DRAKE on page 3 is of course at Petts Wood, which we omitted to mention, while SIR JOHN HAWKINS on page 81 is at Orpington. On page iv the Nelson is not named but the absence of 'LORD NELSON CLASS' under the nameplate means it can only be 850; on page 9 the caption claimed that 858 still sported a plain top chimney – it's a Bulleid one! by way of an additional snippet, on page 48 in the lower photo of 30855 can be seen the plate 'let in' on the smoke deflector where the steam pipe formerly penetrated. This can be seen on some others too, and should not be mistaken for the steampipe itself! (Nothing is easy...)

In the first Lord Nelson *Accompaniment* it has been pointed out that the Bournemouth express headed by LORD HOOD (page 40, upper) is in fact a down train, not an up one.

On page 8 in 'The Book Of' LORD DUNCAN is near Dover not at Folkestone while a little later on page 12 the anonymous location of LORD HOOD turns out to be Petts Wood, though no-one has yet come up with an explanation for the curious 'container' vehicle behind the engine. The train is approaching Petts Wood Junction with the up distant lowered for the spur to Victoria via Bromley. LORD NELSON is on this very spur on page 26. On page 40 we reckoned SIR RICHARD GRENVILLE was running light to Eastleigh shed. It turns out that the photo is taken from the up platform and thus 30853 must be running *from* the shed, *to* the docks. Mr Jeff Dacombe of Seaton also wrote on this matter. LORD HAWKE at Brookwood on page 63 is in fact at Esher; Mr Stevenson: 'the train is travelling *down* on the *up* fast hence the flagman signalling the train'. On page 67 the fairly anonymous location was tentatively put forward as Ashford. Mr Stevenson: 'This is Folkestone Junction up sidings. The signal is the up starter for the southernmost sidings; the chimney was part of a council depot. The signal's finial can be seen above the safety valves of 852 on page 4.'

The boiler list on page 25 of 'The Book' was compiled from the official boiler records. Examination of the Engine Record Cards since has, however, revealed some discrepancies. The necessary adjustments are:
851 change 820 12/59 to 820 9/58
856 change 853 9/58 to 853 11/56
857 change 822 9/58 to 822 3/57
857 add 850 7/60
861 change 856 3/56 to 856 9/54
862 delete 853 7/37
862 change 858 5/54 to 858 6/58
862 delete 820 12/55 and 858 4/61
865 change 852 7/57 to 852 1/56

We are most grateful to all correspondents who took the interest to thoroughly read the books and made the time and effort to write in.